CAMBRIDGE SKILLS FOR FLUENCY
Series Editor: Adrian Doff

Listening 1

Adrian Doff
Carolyn Becket

CAMBRIDGE
UNIVERSITY PRESS

Published by the Press Syndicate of the University of Cambridge
The Pitt Building, Trumpington Street, Cambridge CB2 1RP
40 West 20th Street, New York, NY 10011–4211, USA
10 Stamford Road, Oakleigh, Melbourne 3166, Australia

© Cambridge University Press 1991

First published 1991
Fourth printing 1994

Printed in Great Britain by
Scotprint Ltd, Musselburgh, Scotland

ISBN 0 521 36747 6 book
ISBN 0 521 36544 9 cassette

Copyright
The law allows a reader to make a single copy of part of a book
for purposes of private study. It does not allow the copying of
entire books or the making of multiple copies of extracts. Written
permission for any such copying must always be obtained from the
publisher in advance.

GO

Contents

Acknowledgements

We are very grateful to the following people who have helped in developing this book:
- Tony Lynch for helping us to develop the ideas underlying the book.
- Our editors, Alison Baxter, Jeanne McCarten, Barbara Thomas and Angela Wilde for their consistent support and encouragement.
- Peter Taylor and Studio AVP for their advice and assistance with the recordings and for producing the final cassette.
- The schools who helped in arranging recording sessions, and Margherita Baker for kindly providing the use of her home for some of the recordings.

We would like to thank the following people who contributed to the recordings: Judith Aguda, Margaret Bell, Stephen Bower, Ann Boy, Bryan Cruden, Peter Davison, Shona Grant, John McAuliffe, Desmond Nicholson, Len Nunney, Brian Purvy, Lucy Purvy, Tony Robinson, Ewa Siembieda, Kumiko Thomas, Catherine Walston, Hilary Walston, Martin Whitworth and Kit Woods.

We would also like to thank the teachers at the following institutions, where *Listening 1* was piloted, for all their constructive suggestions without which the improvements in the book would not have been made.

Studio School of English, Cambridge; London School of English, London; Swan School of English, Oxford; Eurocentre, Brighton; Institut Universitaire de Technologie – GEii, Cergy, France; Sydney English Language Centre, Bondi Junction, Australia; Eurocentre, Lee Green, London; Canberra College of Advanced Education, Australia; Klubschule Migros, Bern, Switzerland; Eurocentre, Cambridge.

The authors and publishers are grateful to the following for permission to reproduce copyright material:
J. Allan Cash (pp.14, 17, 36 – parachute, balloon, aeroplane –, 46B, 47); National Tourist Organisation of Greece (p.20 flat); Popperfoto (p.8 Amundsen); Barnaby's Picture Library (p.8 Everest); Sally and Richard Greenhill (p.16); The National Gallery (p.32); The Francis Frith Collection (p.35); The British Tourist Authority Photographic Library (p.36 hang-glider).

The photographs on pp.13, 18, 20 (house), 44 and 46 were taken by Jeremy Pembrey.
Drawings by Tim Beer, Caroline Church, Peter Dennis, Chris Evans, Leslie Marshall and Chris Pavely. Artwork by Hardlines and Peter Ducker.
Book design by Peter Ducker MSTD

Map of the book

Unit	Functional areas	Vocabulary areas	Listening strategies
1 Facts and figures	Stating facts; giving directions; dictating.	Numbers; dates; addresses.	Listening to precise information.
2 Round the world	Guessing; describing location; making suggestions.	Countries; geographical features; tourist sights.	Guessing; listening to precise information.
3 Getting the message	Narration; ability; describing people.	Illness and injury; character adjectives.	Predicting and guessing.
4 Computer dating	Talking about likes and dislikes; expressing preference.	Leisure activities; personal characteristics.	Listening to make a judgement.
5 In the picture	Describing a scene; describing people.	Clothes; everyday objects; action verbs.	Forming a mental picture.
6 Meeting people	Describing people; narration.	Facial features; clothes; parties.	Forming a mental picture; following a story.
7 Rooms	Describing features; location.	Rooms and houses.	Forming a mental picture.
8 Get well soon	Social interaction; giving instructions.	Illness; cures.	Predicting and guessing; following instructions.
9 What's going on?	Social interaction; requests and offers.	Everyday situations.	Predicting and guessing.
10 Early one morning	Describing a scene.	Travel and transport; sight, sound, smell.	Forming a mental picture.

Unit	Functional areas	Vocabulary areas	Listening strategies
11 Presents	Social interaction; narration.	Presents.	Predicting and guessing; following a story.
12 Small talk	Introductions; 'small talk'.	Parties; everyday situations.	Following the 'thread' of a conversation.
13 Van Gogh	Interpreting; imagining.	Paintings; everyday objects.	Matching with your own opinion/ feelings.
14 Two towns	Describing places.	Towns; amenities; agriculture.	Matching with your own experience; forming a mental picture.
15 Air travel	Describing personal experiences; public announcements.	Travel; leisure activities; airports.	Matching with your own experience; listening for specific information.
16 Tarantula	Narration; explanation.	Fears and phobias; spiders; pets.	Following a story; matching with your own knowledge.
17 Customs	Describing routines; sequence.	Customs; activities in the home; festivals.	Following a sequence; matching with your own experience.
18 How to do it	Instructions; sequence.	Making things; using machines.	Following instructions; guessing general meaning.
19 People at work	Describing a routine activity; 'small talk'.	Jobs; transport.	Following the 'thread' of a conversation.
20 Holidays	Describing scenes; narration.	Holidays; travel.	Forming a mental picture; following a description.

1 | Facts and figures

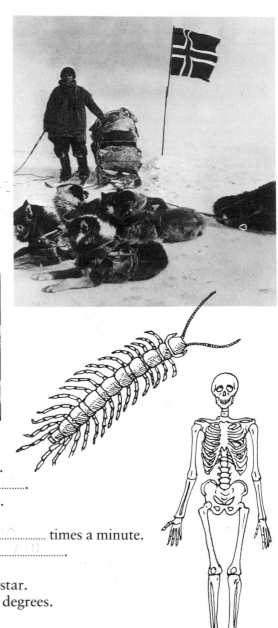

A Numbers

1 🔊 Listen to the numbers, and write them
down. (Some are ordinary numbers,
some are dates.)

a) ....   f) ....
b) ....   g) ....
c) ....   h) ....
d) ....   i) ....
e) ....

2 Write the numbers in the gaps.

1 Mount Everest is .... metres high.
2 Columbus discovered America in ....
3 You have .... bones in your body.
4 A centipede has .... legs.
5 The heart of an average person beats .... times a minute.
6 Amundsen discovered the South Pole in ....
7 A healthy adult has .... teeth.
8 It is .... kilometres to the nearest star.
9 The temperature of the sun is .... degrees.

3 🔊 Listen to the conversations on the tape, and check your answers.

4 **Extension** Think of one or two simple questions like those on the tape, and
write them down.

See if other students can answer your questions.

B Names and addresses

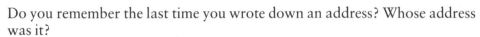

1   When do you write down other people's addresses? When do you give other people your address?

For example:
- you meet someone you like, and you want to contact them again
- you've lost something, and you go to the police

Think of one or two other examples.

Do you remember the last time you wrote down an address? Whose address was it?

2   These addresses have mistakes in them. Listen to the tape, and write the addresses correctly.

3   Listen to each conversation again.

Are the people friends or strangers?
Why are they writing down the address?

4   **Extension**   Tell another student your name, address and telephone number in English. Make sure he/she writes it down correctly.

2 | Round the world

A Guess the country

1   Look at the countries in the picture.

Which ones are in:
- Asia?
- Africa?
- Europe?
- South America?
- Central America?
- the Mediterranean?
- the Caribbean?
- the Atlantic Ocean?
- the Pacific Ocean?

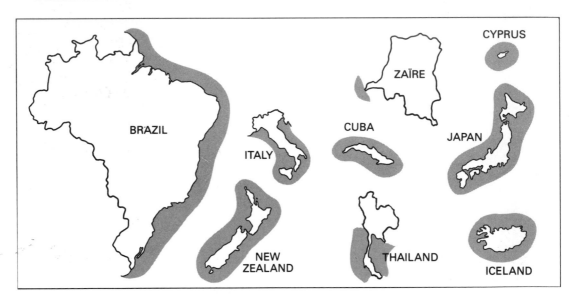

Say two things you know about each country.

Example: Japan is an island.
           In Japan, they make cars and computers.

2   ▭   You will hear three guessing games. One person thinks of a country, and says two or three things about it. The others try to guess the country.

Listen to the tape. Every time there is a pause, try to guess the country.

3   **Extension**   Play the game yourselves.

B Egypt

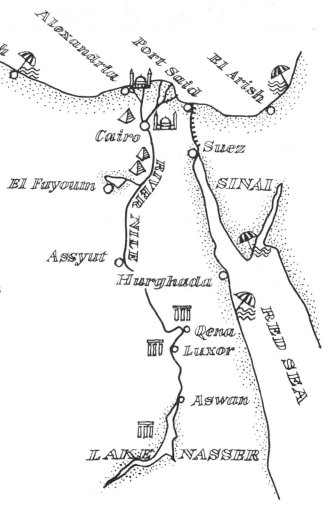

1   Look at the map of Egypt.

Where can you go:
- to see pyramids?
- to see mosques?
- to see ancient temples?
- to go swimming?
- to watch ships?

2   Imagine that you have a few days free in Egypt.

Working with a partner, plan a tour of the country. When you have finished, compare your ideas with other students.

3   [cassette] On the tape, a woman suggests places to visit in Egypt. Listen, and mark the route she suggests on the map.

4   [cassette] You will hear six sentences from the tape. Which places is the woman talking about?

1 ....   4 ....
2 ....   5 ....
3 ....   6 ....

Now listen to the whole conversation again, and check your answers.

5   **Extension**   Choose a country you know fairly well. Make a list of four or five interesting places to visit there.

Then tell another student about the places on your list. Explain why they would be interesting to visit. (*Note:* If possible, use a map to show where the places are.)

3 | Getting the message

A In Florida

1 On the tape, a man describes a recent holiday.
Here are some phrases he uses. What do you
think happened?

in Florida   just drove away
really good   wasn't terribly serious
bumped my head   a good rest
quite nice   a car crash
rather nasty   quite quiet
spoilt the whole holiday
just before I came back
crashed into our car

2 ▭ Now listen to the conversation,
and see if you were right.

B Broken leg

1 A man broke his leg in a climbing accident, and spent a week in hospital. He
has just come home. How is he?

Has he recovered?
Can he walk normally?
What can't he do?
How does he feel?
Does his leg still hurt?

Can you *guess* the answers to these questions?

2 ▭ Listen to the tape line by line. Each time it stops, try to guess what the man
will say next.

3 ▭ Listen to the whole conversation. Now answer the questions in Exercise 1
again.

12

C What's Jean like?

1 These words are all used to describe people.

friendly   boring   mean   interesting   talkative   quiet
outgoing   shy   unfriendly   generous

Match each word with its *opposite*.
Which words do you think are *positive*? Which are *negative*?

2  A woman is talking about an acquaintance called Jean.

Listen to the tape line by line. After each line:

– Put a cross ✗ on the scale, to show how
   much you think she likes or dislikes Jean.
   5 = she likes her a lot,
   0 = she doesn't like her at all.
– Say *why* you think she likes/dislikes her.

	How much does she like Jean? 5 4 3 2 1 0	Why?
Line 1		
Line 2		
Line 3		
Line 4		
Line 5		

3 Listen to the conversation again. In general, how much do you think the
   woman likes Jean?

Which words in Exercise 1 describe Jean best?

4 **Extension**   Look at the words in Exercise 1 again. Write down the *three*
   words that you think describe you best.

Then show what you have written to the person next to you. Try to explain
why you chose those words.

4 | Computer dating

A What are you like?

1 Imagine you answered this advertisement. Below is part of a form sent by Compudate. How would you answer the questions about yourself? (*Do not write anything on the form.*)

Compudate
FIND LOVE WITH
BRITAIN'S FOREMOST
AND LEAST EXPENSIVE
Computer Dating Agency

No matter *where* you live, or *who* you are, COMPUDATE can find you LOCAL introductions . . . all *personally* selected by our experienced staff.

Janice & Dave (Manchester)
"We met after 2 weeks and hope to get married in the Spring of 1991."

SECTION A   ABOUT YOURSELF

1. What is your job (or other occupation)? ....

2. What kind of person are you? (*tick the boxes*)
   ☐ serious?   ☐ shy?   ☐ practical?

3. Which of these do you like? (*tick the boxes*)
   ☐ sports (which?) ....
   ☐ spending time out of doors?   ☐ going out in the evening?
   ☐ going to parties?   ☐ staying at home?

4. Other interests: ....
   ....

2

🔊 Listen to the interview, and complete the form for the woman on the tape.

B Who do you want to meet?

1 Imagine you have gone to Compudate to look for a partner. How would you answer the questions? (*Do not write anything on the form.*)

Compudate

SECTION B   YOUR IDEAL PARTNER

1. What kind of person would you like to meet?

   Age: ....
   Occupation ....

2. Would you prefer someone who is . . .   (*tick the boxes*)

   ☐ serious?

   ☐ shy?

   ☐ fun-loving?

   ☐ well-organised?

   ☐ practical?

   ☐ with a sense of humour?

3. Would you prefer someone who likes . . .
   (*tick the boxes*)

   ☐ going out in the evening?

   ☐ spending time out of doors?

   ☐ staying at home?

   ☐ going to parties?

4. What other interests should the person have? ....

   ....

   ....

---

2 Listen to the interview, and complete the form for the man on the tape.

How well would the woman suit the man?
Do you think the man would suit the woman?

3 **Extension**   Work with another student.

Would the man or the woman suit *you* as a partner?
Which of you would they suit better? Why?

15

5 | In the picture

A Food bowls

1   Look at the picture. Which country do you think it is?

2   Now *cover the picture*.
Try to write six sentences about it from memory. Use the words below.

    old man bowls boy chopsticks rice hat

3   ⌷ On the tape, a man describes the picture from memory. You will hear six sentences. How many are the same as yours?

4   ⌷ Uncover the picture and listen to the complete description.
Is there anything the man gets *wrong* in his description?
Is there anything he leaves out?

16

B In the street

1 Look at the picture on this page *for ten seconds only*. Then cover it. Work with another student. Can you remember what is in it? Together, try to describe it without looking at it.

2   On the tape, a man describes the picture from memory. Listen to eight things he says. Do you think he is right? Write ✓(=Yes), ✗(=No) or ?(=Not sure).

    1 ....

    2 ....

    3 ....

    4 ....

    5 ....

    6 ....

    7 ....

    8 ....

3   Now uncover the picture, and listen to the complete description.

4 **Extension** From your textbook (or any other book you have with you) choose a picture that has a lot of detail in it.

Work with another student. Show your partner the picture for a few seconds only. Then ask him/her to try to describe it from memory.

6 | Meeting people

A Party

1 Imagine you meet these people at a party.

Who looks the most interesting to talk to?
Who looks the least interesting? Why?

2 🔲 You will hear ten remarks. Which of the men in the photos could each one describe?

1	4	7	10 ....
2	5	8	
3	6	9	

3 🔲 You will hear two conversations about the party.

Conversation A
Which person did the woman meet?
Did she like him?

Conversation B
Who did the man talk to?
Did he like him?
What did they talk about?

4 **Extension** Choose any two of the people in the pictures. Imagine you met them at a party. Write three sentences about each of them.

Read out your sentences. See if other students can guess which two people you chose.

18

B First meeting

1 The pictures tell the story of how a man first met his wife. Try to put them in
the correct order.
Can you guess the story?

2   Listen to the story on the tape, and check that you have put the pictures in
the correct order.

3   How many of these questions can you answer?

What was the man writing?   What was the weather like?
What was his friend's name?   What colour clothes was the woman
What kind of party was it?   wearing?
Whose party was it?   Why did she have a suntan?

  Now listen to the tape again, and check your answers.

4 **Extension**   Work with another student. Think of someone you know well
(wife or husband, close friend, boy- or girlfriend).

Tell your partner:
– where you first met them
– how you first met them
– what happened

7 | Rooms

A Rooms with a view

1   Where do you think these buildings are?
Which would you prefer to live in? Why?

A

B

2   🔲   You will hear eight sentences describing rooms in these buildings. Which building could the rooms be in? A or B or both?

1	4	7 ....
2	5	8 ....
3	6	

3   🔲   Now listen to the complete descriptions, and see if you were right.

4   Which speaker uses these words? What does he say?

     wobble   eat   desk   plants   square   trees   sleep
     clock   chairs   central heating

     🔲   Listen again to check your answers.

5   Where do you think each room is in the picture?
Do you think the speaker likes his room?

B A room in Khartoum

1   Try to imagine the main room in this house.

Do you imagine
it to be:
– cool?
– quite warm?
– hot?
– dark?
– full of light?

The room has *wooden shutters* and a *veranda*. Why do you think they are useful?

📼 Now listen to the first part of the tape, and see if you were right.

2   In the next part, the woman talks about the furniture in the room.

Before you listen, try to continue these sentences.

1 Most people use the beds as . . .
2 The beds are very useful because . . .
3 There's a traditional stool beside each chair so that
   you can . . .
4 There are lovely woven woollen rugs, which . . .

📼 Now listen to the tape, and complete the sentences.

3   📼 Listen to the second part again. Imagine the furniture in the room, and mark it on the plan.

4   **Extension**   Work with another student.

Tell him/her about the most unusual room
you have ever stayed in.
Which adjectives in Exercise 1 describe it best?
What furniture did it have?

21

8 | Get well soon

A How do you feel?

A  B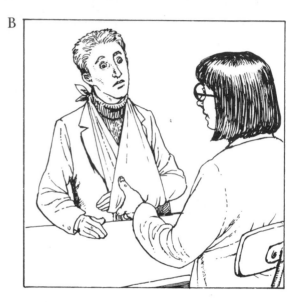

1   Look at the two pictures.

What do you think the woman is saying?
What do you think the man is saying?

2   📼 You will hear twelve remarks.
Listen to each remark, and decide which picture it goes with.

1	5	9 ....
2	6	10 ....
3	7	11 ....
4	8	12 ....

3   📼 Now listen to the two conversations, and check your answers.

4   **Extension**   Work with another student. Choose one of the pictures, and imagine you are the two people in it.

Improvise the conversation. Include language you heard on the tape, but try to add to it and develop the conversation further.

B Cures

1 Which of the things in the pictures might help to cure:

  – a cold?
  – hiccups?

  How could you use them?

2 ▭ Listen to the tape. You will hear four people.

  Which things does each person mention?
  Are they describing a cure for a cold or hiccups?

3 ▭ Listen again, and complete these notes.

  1 First you .... a glass with ....
    Hold your ....
    Take .... from the opposite side of ....

  2 Ask a friend to put .... in your ....
    Drink ....

  3 Undress and ....
    Put .... at the foot of ....
    Drink ...., until you
      ....
      ....

  4 Take a .... and put it in ....
    Undress and wrap ....
    Lie down on ....
    You will soon ....

4 **Extension** Do you know any other cures for colds or hiccups? Write brief instructions like those in Exercise 3. Then show them to another student.

9 | What's going on?

A What really happened?

1   Read these extracts from Peter's diary.

10 November
*We had a party last night, and my cousin Richard came with his new girlfriend, Sarah.
I was just giving Sarah some coffee when I tripped and spilt it on the carpet. Luckily,
it didn't go on her dress, and we all laughed about it.*

15 January
*It was so cold last week – minus 15°! There was a lot of snow about, and the roads
were quite icy. Frieda came to lunch on Friday, and she was so scared of driving
home that she wanted to stay the night with us. I told her not to worry – reports
on the radio said that the roads were quite safe. But she absolutely refused to leave.*

3 March
*Janice's sister has started making dresses... very badly! She sent Janice another
one today, and she tried it on. She wasn't sure if she liked it, but I wanted
to be kind, so I told her it looked really wonderful.*

2   🔲   Peter remembers some things correctly, but not others.

On the tape, you will hear the three conversations which Peter describes in
his diary. Listen, and underline the points where the diary is incorrect.

3   Discuss what really happened. Answer these questions.

Conversation A
What really happened?
How did Sarah feel?
How did Peter feel?
What did he do?

Conversation B
What did Frieda really want to do?
How did Peter feel about it?
What did they say on the radio?

Conversation C
What did Janice really think of the dress?
What did Peter think of it?
What did he say about it?

🔲   Then listen to the tape again, and check your answers.

24

B Requests, offers and invitations

A
> Do let me help you with the washing up.

B
> Could you give me a hand moving this cupboard?

C
> Would you like to come to dinner tonight?

D
> Excuse me, I can't start my car. Do you think you could just help me give it a push?

1   How could you reply to these remarks?
Think of *two* possible replies for each remark, and write them down.

2   🔲 You will hear four replies on the tape. Match them with the remarks.

1 ....   3 ....
2 ....   4 ....

Were any replies the same as yours?

3   🔲 Now listen to the complete conversations, and fill in the gaps.

A. I asked her to help me move the cupboard, but she couldn't because ....
So we decided to ....

B. I invited him to dinner tonight, but he couldn't come because ....
So he's .... instead.

C. I asked him to help me push my car. At first, he didn't want to because ....
Finally he ....

D. I offered to help her with the washing up, but she ....
Instead, she asked me to ....

4   **Extension**   Work with another student. Can you remember a time recently when someone asked you for help or offered to help you?
Tell your partner what happened.

10 | Early one morning

A The moment of waking

1 Think of a time when you slept while you were travelling: on a bus, a train, a plane, a boat, or in a car.

Try to remember the moment when you woke up.
Where were you? What was it like? How did you feel?
Use the words below to help you talk about it.

It was:
   stuffy   chilly   draughty
   smelly   dark   light

I felt:
   tired   stiff   refreshed   excited
   hot   cold   hungry   thirsty

2 ▮▮ You will hear a woman talking about waking up on a train.
Listen, and underline the words in Exercise 1 that fit her description.

3 Complete these sentences.

When she woke up, she thought she could
   smell ...., but in fact it was the
   smell of ....
She heard a noise like a ...., which
   was actually the noise of ....
The floor seemed to be ....
Her back was .... because she was
   lying on ....

4 Here is a plan of the compartment, as seen from above.

▮▮ Listen to the last part of the tape again.
On the plan, show how the people
were sleeping.

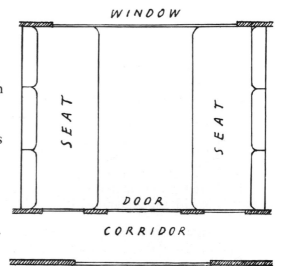

26

B Sights, sounds and smells

1 Imagine that you wake up in a strange place, and you are aware of these things.

Try to imagine the scene.
— Where do you think you are?
— Imagine the things above. Which can you *see*? Which can you *hear*? Which can you *smell*?

2   On the tape, a woman describes the scene. Which things does she see, hear and smell? Tick the correct spaces in the table.

	She sees . . .	She hears . . .	She smells . . .
a bell			
rushing water			
engines			
bacon and eggs			
mist			
people drinking tea			

Where do you think the woman was?

3 How many of these questions can you answer?

1 What time of day was it?
2 Where was she sleeping?
3 Did she like the noise?
4 Did she stay in bed?
5 What did she see?
6 What was it like outside?
7 What was it like inside?

  Now listen to the sentences on the tape, and check your answers.

4 **Extension** What is the most unusual place you have ever slept in? Make a list of things you saw, heard and smelt as you woke up.

Show your list to another student, and tell him/her about it.

11 | Presents

A Envelope

1   It is your birthday.
Someone gives you this
envelope.

Try to imagine what
might be inside it. Make
a list.

Show your list to another
student.
Which of the things in
your list would you most
like as a birthday
present?

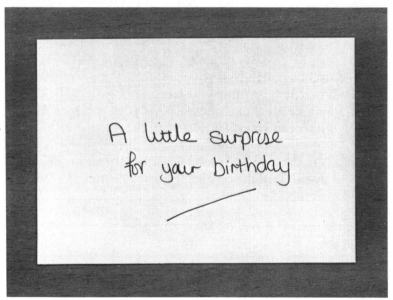

*A little surprise
for your birthday*

2   On the tape, a man is opening an envelope like the one in the picture. He uses
the words below.

    big   ridiculous   card   fortune   cost   Bombay

Can you guess what is in the envelope?
What do you think the man says?

3   Listen to the tape, and answer the questions.

   What *is* in the envelope?
   What does the man think of it?
   What will he do?
   What will the woman do?

4   **Extension**   Think of an interesting present, and write it on a piece of paper.
Fold the paper over, and give it to another student.

When you receive your 'present', open it and say what you think of it.

B Presents for the family

You will hear a story about a girl who went to stay in France.

1 🔊 Listen to the first line of the story.

How do you think the story
continues? Use the outline in the
box.

🔊 Listen again, and see if you were
right.

> I took with me some . . .
> . . . and gave them to . . .

2 🔊 Now listen to the next line of the
story.

How do you think the story
continues? Use the outline in the
box.

🔊 Listen again, and see if you were
right.

> At the end of my stay I went . . .
> . . . and I bought . . .
> . . . to take back to . . .

3 🔊 Now listen to the next line of the
story.

How do you think the story
continues? Use the outline in the
box.

🔊 Listen again, and see if you were
right.

> So I opened . . .
> . . . and I was standing . . .
> . . . with a . . .
> . . . when the lady of the house . . .

4 Try to guess how the story ends.

What did the lady of the house say?
How did the speaker feel?
What did she do?

🔊 Now listen to the last part of the story.

5 **Extension**   Imagine you are going to stay with a family abroad.

Think of two or three interesting presents to take from your own country to
give them at the end of your stay.

Work with another student. Imagine this student is the person you have been
staying with. Give him/her your 'presents', and explain what they are.

12 | Small talk

A Party guests

1 What do you think the people in the pictures are saying?

2 🔲 Listen to the tape, and look at the pictures.

  – Which is: (a) John? (b) Christian? (c) Adrienne?
  – Complete the gaps in the bubbles.

3 🔲 Listen again, and write down everything you know about the three people.

John	Christian	Adrienne
....	....	....
....	....	....
....	....	....

B Coffee morning

1   On the tape, you will hear some people chatting.

Cover this page below the line.

🔲   Listen to the tape, and try to answer these questions.

How many people are there?
Have they just arrived or are they about to leave?
When are they going to meet again?

Now uncover the page.

---

2   Here are some phrases from the conversation.
Before you listen again, try to put them in the correct order.

3   🔲   Now listen to the tape again. Is the order the same as you thought?

13 | Van Gogh

A Van Gogh's chair

1 Look at this picture by Van Gogh.

  1 Do you think the picture is:
    – very interesting?
    – fairly interesting?
    – not at all interesting?
    Can you say why?

  2 Do you know what colour Van Gogh painted:
    – the chair?
    – the walls?
    – the tiled floor?
    If not, can you guess?

  3 What does the picture tell us about the man who uses this chair? Choose
    the sentences you agree with.

    He's old.   He's lonely.
    He's a heavy smoker.   He has gone away for ever.
    He's poor.   He'll be back soon.
    He's rich.

2   ▭ You will hear a woman talking about the picture. How would *she* answer
   the questions above?

32

B Your own chair

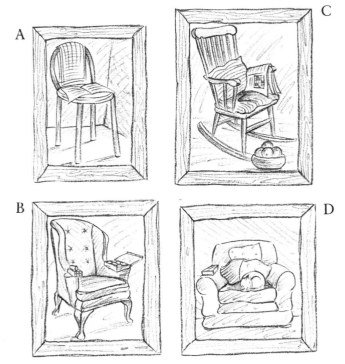

A

C

B

D

1 Four people imagine a picture in the style of Van Gogh showing their own chair.

Look at the pictures, and decide which person:

- likes to be comfortable
- likes cooking
- likes eating
- likes animals
- likes watching television
- likes doing crossword puzzles
- smokes

2 ▭ Listen to the tape, and match the descriptions with the pictures.

1 ....   3 ....
2 ....   4 ....

3 Which speaker uses these words?

   a rocking chair   a tea-towel   remote control   a squeak

What exactly do they say?

▭ Listen to the sentences on the tape, and check your answers.

4 **Extension**   Imagine you are painting a picture of your own chair. Think of two things to put on it, which show something about you.

Tell another student what you have chosen, and explain why.

14 | Two towns

A Street scene

1 Imagine walking down the main street of your home town. Make a list of things you can *see*, *hear* and *smell*.

Sights	Sounds	Smells

Read out your list to your partner.

Which sights, sounds and smells in your town are pleasant?
Which are unpleasant?

2 🎧 On the tape, a man describes a town. Listen and note down the things he saw, heard and smelt.

Sights	Sounds	Smells

3 What kind of town do you think the man is talking about?
Is it big or small? Quiet or noisy?
Where do you think the town is? In what kind of country?

B A town in Wales

1 Look at the picture of Builth Wells.

Do you think it looks:

pretty?   ugly?   beautiful?
grey?   colourful?   busy?
friendly?   noisy?   quiet?

📼 Listen to the first part of the tape.

1 Which words from the list above did the woman use?
2 Do you think she likes the town?

2 On the second part of the tape, the woman talks about Builth Wells market. Before you listen, read this summary. Can you guess the missing words?

On Mondays the farmers bring .... to the market. In the old days, they drove the .... through the ...., but nowadays they usually use .... But you can still see hundreds of .... being chased through the .... to the .... It's incredibly ....

📼 Now listen, and fill in the missing words.

3 Would you recommend Builth Wells to someone who says:

– 'I want to go to a place with lots of tourists.'
– 'I want to go somewhere quiet where I can be alone.'
– 'I want to meet Welsh people.'
– 'I'd like to stay somewhere picturesque.'
– 'I'm interested in buying sheep.'

What would you tell each person about the town?

4 **Extension** Think of a town you know well. Write a list of words that describe it best.

Show your list to another student and find out as much as you can about the town he/she chose.

Find out: what it is like now, what it was like in the past, what kind of people visit it, and why.

15 | Air travel

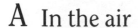

A In the air

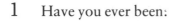

1 Have you ever been:

- – in a small aeroplane?
- – in a balloon?
- – parachuting?
- – hang-gliding?

2 Choose *one*. Try to imagine the experience. Write three sentences about it.

Example:
I was terrified.
I kept my eyes closed all the time.
It was very cold and windy.

3 ▭ On the tape, you will hear four people talking. What is each person describing? How do you know?

Speaker A: .... Speaker C: ....
Speaker B: .... Speaker D: ....

Did they say the same things as you?

4 How many questions can you answer?

Speaker A
1 Did she enjoy it?
2 How did she feel?
3 What could she see?

Speaker C
1 How did he take off?
2 What could he see?
3 How long did it last?

Speaker B
1 How did she feel?
2 How did it start?
3 What did she do later?

Speaker D
1 Who was he with?
2 What was it like?
3 What was the landing like?

5 ▭ You will hear sentences from the tape. Listen, and check your answers.

B Airport

1

```
        Flight          Date          Gato
        Vol             Data          Porte
        Flug            Datum         Ausgang

  ┌─────────────────────────────────┐    ⊛ PAN AM.
  │ PA 241/0314 29 FEB G56 │
  └─────────────────────────────────┘         BOARDING PASS
   No Smoking    Smoking                     CARTE D'ACCES A BORD
      Seat         Seat        Class            BORDKARTE
  ⊘  Siege    ⊖  Siege       Cabine
      Sitz         Sitz        Klasse
  ┌─────────────────────────────────┐
  │ 78B  269              Y │
  └─────────────────────────────────┘
  ┌─────────────────────────────────┐
  │ LHR/JFK                          │
  │        From—Da—Von/To—A—Nach     │
  │ UNDERHILL/JMISS                  │
  └─────────────────────────────────┘
              Name—Nom—Name
     SEE REVERSE SIDE FOR IMPORTANT INFORMATION
```

You are Joanne Underhill. You are travelling on a Pan American flight to New York this afternoon, and you are waiting in the departure lounge.

▭ You will hear seven announcements.
Which announcements concern you?
What should you do about them?

Complete the table.

✓ or ✗	*What should you do?*
1	
2	
3	
4	
5	
6	
7	

2   Imagine that the person sitting next to you cannot hear very well.

▭ Listen to the announcements again. After each one, explain to him/her what it is about.

16 | Tarantula

A One day in California . . .

1 Which of these words go with the picture?

friendly   hairy
bite   black
poisonous   harmless
pet   spider
dangerous

What other words could describe a tarantula?

2 Here are extracts from two stories:

During my stay in America, I often went for long walks in the country. One morning, when I was out walking, I came upon a huge tarantula, sitting absolutely still in the middle of the path . . .

I was working as a teacher in West Africa. One night, I was sitting in bed reading a book, when I noticed a large black spider crawling across the bed towards me . . .

Imagine this happened to *you*. What would you do?

Would you:
— run away?
— try to kill the tarantula? (How?)
— keep still?
— pick the tarantula up?
— . . .?

3   Listen to the tape. What does the man do? Why?

4 Here are some words from the story. What do they mean?

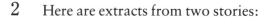

sandhills   gently   jogging   California   brave   bear
giant   hurt

   Listen to the tape again. What exactly does the man say?

B Fear of spiders

1 Here are some facts about tarantulas. Which do you think are true? Write 'yes' or 'no' in column A.

	A	B
Tarantulas are the biggest of all spiders.		
Black widow spiders are more dangerous than tarantulas.		
Tarantulas can bite.		
Tarantulas are poisonous.		
Pet rabbits are more dangerous than tarantulas.		
Most snakes are poisonous.		—
Most spiders are poisonous.		—

2 🔲 Listen to the tape. What does the woman say about tarantulas? Write 'yes' or 'no' in column B.

3 In the next part of the tape, the speaker talks about spiders and snakes. Before you listen, read what she says. Can you guess the missing words?

People are .... of spiders and they are
.... of snakes. And obviously some spiders and some
snakes really are .... But most snakes are
................................, and it's really strange that people are so
.... of spiders, because it's difficult to find a spider that's
really ....

🔲 Now listen, and fill in the missing words.

Look again at Exercise 1. Can you answer the last two questions?

4 Look at this notice. What is it?
Where might you see it?
Do you find it surprising? Why?

🔲 Now listen to the last part
of the tape.

17 | Customs

A Japanese bath

1 What do you do when you have a bath? Put these actions in the correct order for you. (Write numbers in column A.)

	A	B
Get dressed.		
Heat the water.		
Get out of the bath.		
Fill the bath with water.		
Wash yourself.		
Get undressed.		
Rinse yourself.		
Get in the bath.		
Wash your hair.		
Dry yourself.		
Sit in the bath and relax.		
....		
....		

Do you do anything else? Add it to the list.

2 🔲 You will hear someone talking about a Japanese bath. Listen, and put the actions in the correct order. (Write numbers in column B.)

3 Which of these is a traditional Japanese bath?
Why do you think so?

B Christmas in Poland

1   Can you answer these questions?

> When is Christmas Eve?
> Where might you find a Christmas tree?
> What are Christmas carols?

2   Here are some things that people do on Christmas Eve in Poland. What order do you think they should be in? (Write numbers in the column.)

Sit at the table.	
Wish each other good luck.	
Eat a special meal.	
Go to church.	
Sing Christmas carols.	
Break wafers.	
Open Christmas presents.	

    You will hear a woman talking about Christmas in Poland. Listen, and put the events in the correct order.

3   How many of these questions can you answer?

1   What is the most important event on Christmas Eve?
2   How many dishes are there?
3   How many should you eat?
4   Why?
5   Where are the Christmas presents?
6   When do people go to church?

    Now listen to the sentences on the tape, and check your answers.

4   **Extension**   Work with another student, and discuss the following questions together.

Do people celebrate Christmas Eve in your country? If so, what do people do on Christmas Eve?
What things are the same as in Poland? What things are different?
If people in your country don't celebrate Christmas, what is the main religious feast day? How do people celebrate it?

18 | How to do it

A Origami

1 How to make a jumping frog . . .
   Take a piece of paper, about 10 cm. × 10 cm. It must be exactly square.

   🔲 Listen and follow the instructions.

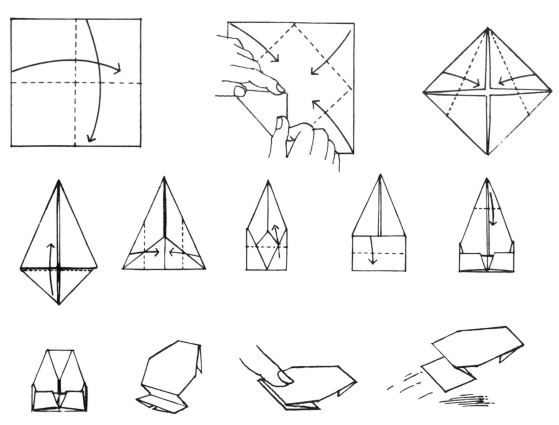

2 **Extension** Do you know how to make anything else from folding paper?

   If you do:
   — sit with a group of four or five other students
   — ask them all to take a piece of paper
   — show them what to do, giving instructions in English

B Press this button . . .

1   ⌨   You will hear four people giving instructions for using things.

Listen, and guess what the people are talking about. What words did you hear that helped you decide?

2   ⌨   Listen again. This time you will hear the instructions again, and also the sound of someone following the instructions.

What are the people doing?

3   Look at the words below. Use a dictionary to check the meaning of any you are not sure about.

Nouns: lid   knob   key   keyboard   keyhole   thumb
               back   wood   saw   carrot   accelerator   fingers

Verbs: push   pull   turn   press

4   ⌨   Listen to the tape again, and use the words to complete these notes.

1 Put the .... on and .... it till it clicks.
Put the .... in the funnel.
.... the .... to the right.

2 Hold the .... down hard on the table.
Put the .... against the mark on the ....
.... it slowly towards you, then .... it
back gently.

3 Put the .... in the ....
.... it once.
.... it again and .... down on the
....

4 Sit with your .... straight and your ....
out in front of you.
Put your right .... over the middle of the
....
Put your left .... in the same place.

19 | People at work

A A working day

1 You will hear someone describing a typical day's work. He uses the words below.

window   hole   glass   paint
weather coat   lunchtime

What do you think his job is? Put the words together to make a story.

2 🔲 Listen to the tape. What is his job? What did he do during the day?

3 🔲 You will hear another person describing a typical day's work.

Listen, and decide which of these is his job:
– He gives language tests to foreign students.
– He interviews people who want to join the police.
– He gives people driving tests.
– He tests cars to see if they are safe.

How did you decide?

4 🔲 Listen again, and complete the table.

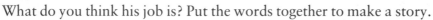

	Pass/Fail	What happened?
1	....	....
2	....	–
3	....	–
4	....	–
5	....	....

5 **Extension** Think of any job, and imagine it is yours. Imagine five things you did yesterday as part of your job, and write them down. Read out your sentences to another student. See if he/she can guess what your job is.

B Round the table

1   Look at the picture, and guess the answers to these questions.

    1 Where are these people? Why are they here?
    2 Who is still missing?
       Why isn't (s)he here yet?
    3 What are the people talking about?

2   Listen to the tape, and answer the questions again.

3   Listen to the conversation again. Every time the tape stops, answer one of
the questions below.

    1 Late for what? 'Terrible' in what way?
    2 Started what?
    3 What was bad?
    4 What does 'jammed' mean?
    5 Tried to avoid what? What sort of 'jam'?
    6 Who? In the middle of what?
    7 What do they decide to do? Why?

20 | Holidays

A Holiday photos

1   You will hear people talking about these holiday photos. What countries do you think they show?

2   Which of these words do you think go with each picture?

      mountain   charcoal   tea   lamb   kebabs   pushchair
      daughter   breakfast

3   Choose two words for each picture. Try to make a sentence about the picture. For example:

      Picture C: This is my *daughter* in a *pushchair*.

4   🔊   Listen to the sentences on the tape, and match them with the pictures.

      1 ....   2 ....   3 ....   4 ....
      5 ....   6 ....

5   🔊   Now listen to the complete descriptions.

      Picture A: Where is it?
                      What did the speaker do next?

      Picture B: Where is it?
                      Who are the people in the photo?

      Picture C: Where are the speaker's children?
                      Who do you think took the photo?

B The Seychelles

1   What do you know about the Seychelles?

Work with other students, and make a list of:
– things you know, e.g. they are islands
– things you are not sure of, e.g. people speak French there(?)

2   ▭   On the tape you will hear a woman talking about a holiday in the Seychelles. Listen, and mark her route on the map.

3   ▭   Listen again. Which islands would you recommend to someone who says:

– 'I want complete peace and quiet.'
– 'I'm very interested in birds, animals and plants.'
– 'I'd like to go snorkelling.'
– 'I want to go somewhere with plenty of shops and a good night life.'

4   Imagine you could spend a week on one of the islands the woman mentions. Which would you choose? Why?

5   **Extension**   Work with another student. Find out if your partner has ever been to an island.

Find out:
– where it was
– when he/she went there
– what he/she did there
– what it was like

Tapescript

Unit 1 Facts and figures

1A Numbers

EXERCISE 1

a) 32   f) 5,500
b) 206   g) 1492
c) 100,000   h) 70
d) 350   i) 1911
e) 8,848

EXERCISE 3

1 A: Do you know how many teeth you've
      got?
   B: How many teeth? Ooh, ooh . . . 24?
      More? (*A: Yes*) 32?
   A: Yes.

2 A: Do you know how many bones there are
      in your body?
   B: How many bones? I'll take a guess. 153.
   A: 206.

3 A: How far away is the nearest star?
   B: I've no idea. How far is it?
   A: 100,000 kilometres.
   B: Is it really?

4 A: Do you know how many legs a centipede
      has?
   B: It sounds to me as if it's got a hundred.
   A: No. (*B: Really?*) 350.

5 A: Guess how high Mount Everest is.
   B: Um – let me think. Um – 10,000 metres?
   A: Very close. It's actually 8,848 metres.

6 A: Can you guess how hot the sun is?
   B: It's, er, 3,000 degrees centigrade.
   A: No, much more than that. It's 5,500
      degrees centigrade.

7 A: Do you know when Columbus
      discovered America?
   B: Yes, I think I do. It was 1492, wasn't it?
   A: Yes, that's right.

8 A: How often does your heart beat?
   B: 98 times a minute.
   A: No, 70 times a minute.

9 A: What year did Amundsen reach the South
      Pole?
   B: Oh, um, 1883?
   A: 1911.

1B Names and addresses

EXERCISES 2 and 3

1 A: Well, look, we must keep in touch.
   B: Let me give you my address.
   A: Right – OK.
   B: John Mitchell.
   A: John Mitchell. Is that two L's?
   B: Yes. M–I–T–C–H–E–double L.
      (*A: Right*) And the address is fifteen
      (*A: Fifteen*) Brougham Place . . .
   A: Brougham. B–R . . . How do you spell
      Brougham?
   B: B–R–O–U–G–H–A–M.
   A: Ah yes. Ridiculous.
   B: And that's Oxford. (*A: Right, um*) I'll
      give you my telephone number.
      (*A: Telephone number, yep*) 223.
      (*A: 223*) 6790.
   A: 6790. Right. Right, I'll give you a ring.

2 A: Look, I've got a friend in Singapore. You
      could call on him if you've got time. Do
      you want his address?
   B: Yes, I'd love it, thank you.
   A: Well, his name is Joe Harding. J–O–E
      Harding H–A–R–D–I–N–G. And the
      address is The Manhattan Building,
      (*B: Manhattan?*) Manhattan (*B: The
      Manhattan Building*) 2563 Orchard
      Road . . .
   B: That was 2563? (*A: Yes, that's right*)
      Orchard Road.
   A: Singapore. (*B: Singapore*) And the
      telephone number is 236 47539.

B: I've got it.

3 A: There's a very good travel agent that I always go to, and I'm sure they'd find you a cheap flight to America. Um, I'll give you the address, shall I? (*B: Oh, thanks*) It's Solair Travel.

B: Sorry, how do you spell that?

A: S–O–L–A–I–R Travel, (*B: Right*) 15A Merman Street . . .

B: 15A – was that Merman Street?

A: Yes, M–E–R–M–A–N Street, (*B: Right, got that*) Edinburgh. And, I mean you could call in if you like.

B: Whereabouts is it?

A: It's just off George Street. You probably know it, it's round the corner from the King's Theatre. (*B: Oh yes*) You know it. Well, just go in and ask for Mr Mackay.

Unit 2   Round the world

2A   *Guess the country*

EXERCISE 2

1 – This country is an island, and it has a very small population, and most of the population live in the capital city. ●
– Is it a very dry country?
– Um – no. ●
– Is it in the Caribbean?
– No it isn't. ●
– Is it in the Pacific?
– No. ●
– Is it in Europe? (*Uh, huh*)
– Is it divided into two halves?
– No. ●
– Is it very popular for tourists?
– Not really, no. ●
– Is it in the Mediterranean?
– No. ●
– Is it in the Atlantic?
– Um, yes, I think so. ●
– It's not Iceland, is it?
– Yes.

2 – This country is quite a large country. It has changed its capital since the Second World War, and it's famous for its jungles. ●
– Is it an African country?
– No it isn't. ●
– Is it a South American country?
– Yes. ●
– Sorry, did you say it was large or small?
– Er, pretty large. (*large*) ●
– Does it have a newly built capital?

– Yes, it does. ●
– Brazil?
– Brazil. That's correct.

3 – This is a small country. It's mountainous and it has a small population. ●
– Is it in Europe?
– No. ●
– Is it in Asia?
– No. ●
– South America?
– No. ●
– Africa?
– No. ●
– North America?
– No. ●
– Is it a hot country?
– Slightly hotter than Britain. ●
– Does it have a dry climate or . . .?
– No it has a very wet climate. ●
– A small population, you said?
– Yes. ●
– Is it an island country?
– Yes. ●
– Divided into two islands?
– Yes. ●
– Is it New Zealand?
– Yes.

2B   *Egypt*

EXERCISE 3

A: Where are the best places in Egypt?

B: Well, Cairo's very interesting, but it's very busy and it would be very hot in the summer. The best time to go is really in winter, and then it's wonderful to travel up the Nile. I really enjoyed going by train. You just look at the view all the way along. And when you get up to Qena, there's a very beautiful temple called Dendera.

A: Where's Qena?

B: Qena's just before you get to Luxor . . .

A: And then of course Luxor, there's the Valley of the Kings and the Temple in Luxor – there's a lot to see. And then from, in fact from Qena you can take the bus over to the Red Sea, and travel back along the coast.

B: What's it like, this coast?

A: It's not really quite so nice, it's, er . . . it wouldn't be a very good place to go for a seaside holiday, the best place to go for good beaches and for the sea is on the other side of Sinai, on the Gulf of Aqaba.

And Suez itself is not a very nice town at all – it's very industrial, it's got a lot of factories. But Port Said, you can go from Suez to Port Said, which is back on the Mediterranean coast, and Port Said's a fascinating place, it's very interesting, and you can watch all the boats going into the canal. And then from there you can easily take a bus back to Cairo.

EXERCISE 4

1 It's very interesting, and you can watch all the boats going into the canal.
2 You just look at the view all the way along.
3 It wouldn't be a very good place to go for a seaside holiday.
4 It's very industrial, it's got a lot of factories.
5 It's very busy and it would be very hot in the summer.
6 There's a very beautiful temple called Dendera.

Unit 3   Getting the message

3A   In Florida

EXERCISE 2

A: So what did you do on your holiday?
B: Oh it was really good. I was in Florida, you see. Um . . . Well . . . it was quite quiet, I mean I didn't do an awful lot, but I had a good rest . . . Yeah – it was quite nice . . . The only thing was that just before I came back I was involved in a car crash. (*Oh*) Oh, it wasn't terribly serious, I just bumped my head a bit, but um . . . Well, it, you know, it was rather nasty, and the person who crashed into our car just – just drove away and didn't stop. And somehow that spoilt the whole holiday, really.

3B   Broken leg

EXERCISE 2

A: I heard you hadn't been well. What happened?
B: Oh, ●
    oh, I'm not too bad now. I'm out of hospital anyway. Well, at least ●
    Well, at least I'm walking again. ●
    I have to be a bit careful still. I mean, I can't ●
    I can't walk very far or ●
    Or go upstairs or – or anything like that. And I ●

And I get tired very very easily, so – well, to be honest, I'm feeling ●
I'm feeling a bit depressed really, because ●
Because this leg still really hurts.

EXERCISE 3

A: I heard you hadn't been well. What happened?
B: Oh I'm not too bad now. I'm out of hospital anyway. Well, at least I'm walking again. I have to be a bit careful still. I mean, I can't walk very far or go upstairs or anything like that. And I get tired very very easily, so – well, to be honest, I'm feeling a bit depressed really, because this leg still really hurts.

3C   What's Jean like?

EXERCISE 2

A: So what's Jean like?
B: Oh, she's very nice – she's very friendly. ●
    I've always got on quite well with her. ●
    Um, the only thing is she does tend to talk quite a lot. ●
    You know, she's one of those people who just goes on and on and on, and you know it's hard to stop her once she starts talking. ●
    I find her quite boring sometimes, actually.

EXERCISE 3

A: So what's Jean like?
B: Oh, she's very nice – she's very friendly. I've always got on quite well with her. Um, the only thing is she does tend to talk quite a lot. You know, she's one of those people who just goes on and on and on, and you know it's hard to stop her once she starts talking. I find her quite boring sometimes, actually.

Unit 4   Computer dating

4A   What are you like?

EXERCISE 2

A: What's your job?
B: Well at the moment I'm working for a private language school as an administrator.
A: What kind of person would you say that you are? For example, are you serious?
B: No, I don't think I'm very serious. I really enjoy having a good time, laughing.
A: Are you shy?

B: Yes, I would say so.

A: Would you say that you were a practical person, for example are you good with your hands?

B: That's a difficult question. A lot of people say I'm practical, but I don't think I'm very mechanical. I wouldn't be very good at mending machines.

A: Now I'd like to find out what you like doing in your spare time, so if I could ask you a few questions about that. (*B: Yes, please do*)

A: Do you do any sports?

B: Er, yes, I dance, I'm very fond of modern dance, and I like swimming, jogging.

A: Do you enjoy the countryside?

B: Very much.

A: Is there anything else you particularly like doing?

B: Um, I love travelling, and I'm very fond of music. I play the piano and I enjoy listening to music too.

4B *Who do you want to meet?*

EXERCISE 2

A: Mr Thompson, what kind of person would you like to meet?

B: Well, I want somebody who's not too old, probably around, say, 22, could be a bit younger, I don't mind. Um, somebody also that has a sense of humour, um she must be quite attractive, and like spending her time outside, and visiting things.

A: What sort of job do you think she should have?

B: Now that's a bit difficult to say, but probably she will be in some kind of profession. It could be in working in a hospital, could be a teacher.

A: What kind of people do you like? For example, do you like serious people? Or do you like shy people? Or do you like people who are good at working with their hands?

B: Shy people are always difficult to get on with. I think I'd rather have someone who's relatively open and fun-loving.

A: And a practical person?

B: Yes, I think this person must be able to help about the house or the flat or whatever, and must be organised to a certain extent.

A: What sort of things do you think she should like doing?

B: Well, I think if she likes outdoor sports, for example tennis, swimming, um also I think she has to like music, go to concerts,

generally things that I'm interested in. I'm probably being a little bit selfish.

Unit 5   In the picture

5A *Food bowls*

EXERCISE 3

1 An old man is sitting at a table.
2 And on the table there are five or six bowls.
3 There's a small boy at the far side of the table.
4 The old man is holding a pair of chopsticks.
5 He's helping himself to some rice which is in a bowl.
6 The old man is, is, er, is wearing a hat.

EXERCISE 4

Um . . . an old man is sitting at a table and on the table there are five or six bowls and er . . . there's a small boy at the far side of the table, um, who is probably standing, not sitting, but standing and looking up onto the table but we can only see half of his face and he's looking at the old man, um. The old man is holding a pair of chopsticks and he's helping himself to some rice which is in a bowl which he is holding and in the bowls on the table there is also some rice. The old man is, is er . . . is wearing a hat, rather large hat, black, um, and, er, a robe, of some sort. I think this is in perhaps, China, perhaps, um, Tibet or somewhere like that.

5B *In the street*

EXERCISE 2

1 A lady is standing in the street.
2 There's a bicycle near her.
3 And she's holding a piece of material with flowers on it.
4 She's wearing a long robe and also headgear which almost entirely covers her face.
5 I think only her eyes are, are visible.
6 She's looking to one side as if she's perhaps waiting for, expecting somebody to, to, er, to arrive.
7 Behind her there are, um, there are some shops, um, and there are people looking in the shops.
8 Probably, um, this is in the, in the Middle East or maybe Nor . . . North Africa.

EXERCISE 3

A lady is standing in the street. There's a bicycle near her and she's holding a piece of material with flowers on it. She's wearing a long robe and also headgear which almost entirely covers her face, in fact I think only her eyes are, are visible. Um, she's looking to one side as if she's perhaps waiting for, expecting somebody to, to er, to arrive. Behind her there are, um, there are some shops, um, and there are people looking in the shops. It could be in a market perhaps or a busy street. Probably, um, this is in the, in the Middle East or maybe Nor . . . North Africa.

Unit 6   Meeting people

6A   Party

EXERCISE 2

1 He had thick, brown, wavy hair.
2 He had a beard and a moustache.
3 He had quite a long face.
4 He had spectacles.
5 He had dark hair and a dark pullover.
6 He was wearing a check shirt.
7 He had a sort of whitish shirt.
8 He had a blue scarf.
9 He looked like an unhappy dog.
10 He's a teacher.

EXERCISE 3

A) A: How did you enjoy the party?
    B: Oh it was great, wasn't it?
    A: It was lovely. What did you think of Jeff?
    B: Jeff.
    A: Um, you can't remember him? He had thick brown wavy hair and a beard, a moustache, and spectacles – you don't remember?
    B: I don't think I do, actually.
    A: He was wearing a check shirt – sort of red and black check, and a blue scarf. (B: Ooh) He was really nice.
    B: What does he do?
    A: He's a teacher. (B: Uuh)

B) A: What a great party.
    B: You think so? I thought it was dreadful. I got stuck in the corner with this bloke.
    A: What was he like?
    B: What was he like? Well, he had quite a long face – it looked rather like an unhappy dog. Dark hair, dark pullover, a sort of whitish shirt . . . And he talked all the time about roads, driving between his home and his mother-in-law's, which was the best road to take. Can you imagine? When he wasn't

talking about roads, he was talking about the weather. I mean he was so boring.

6B   First meeting

EXERCISES 2 and 3

I was working on a report in a little office, when a friend of mine, Richard, came by and said 'I'm having a birthday party tonight. Will you come?' And his house was very close to where I was working.

It was a balmy summer's evening, and I made my way up this tall building – his house – and made my way to the roof, where lots of people were gathered.

And immediately I got up there, I bumped into this lady, who was wearing a dress which was a flower design, of beautiful red design, and she had tights, I remember, which were light red as well, which at the time were slightly unusual. She had very close-cropped hair, and a tan – a rather attractive suntan.

And she was taking round some drinks to people, and she handed me a drink. And we immediately got talking about where she'd been on holiday, which was in Spain. And that was the beginning of a very enjoyable relationship.

Unit 7   Rooms

7A   Rooms with a view

EXERCISE 2

1 The house is about 300 years old.
2 There's a desk looking out over a street.
3 We have a lovely view from the balcony.
4 It's a good room to live in in the summer.
5 We sit on the balcony a lot, almost live on it.
6 I live in a small flat, on the sixth floor of a high building.
7 There are two armchairs.
8 I can't see any trees from the window.

EXERCISES 3 and 4

A) The house is about 300 years old, and the room is not exactly square or modern. In the room there's a desk looking out over a street – I can't see any trees from the window, I can just see the houses the other side. Yeah, the desk looks out through the window. There are two armchairs – they both wobble because the floor's not even, and there's a grandfather clock in one corner. It's a good room to live in in the

52

summer. There's no central heating, so in the winter it's bitterly cold.

B) I live in a small flat on the sixth floor of a high building, and so we have a lovely view from the balcony. We have a big balcony with a lot of plants and chairs and tables on the balcony – we sit on the balcony a lot, almost live on it, eat on it, sleep on it sometimes. But it's the balcony that I took the flat for in the first place. I saw the flat, and then I saw the balcony and I thought 'Yes'.

7B   A room in Khartoum

EXERCISE 1

It's a lovely room, it's L-shaped, and very cool because of the shutters, the wooden shutters. In a way – er – you would think that the room wasn't pleasant because it's dark, but since it's so very hot outside it's a great relief to come into a cool dark sort of place. And it has a veranda, and this is a very nice thing to have because it gives you lots more room in the house in fact to spread your things about, and you can leave things there quite safely.

EXERCISES 2 and 3

In the room we have some beds which most people use as settees, and you can use these and put lots and lots of cushions on them. They're very useful – you can move them around and use them for all sorts of things. Very little furniture, really – just a bookcase and the traditional stool beside each chair, so that you can have your drinks, because obviously in a hot place you need lots to drink, so every chair has its own little drink stool beside it. And in the other bit of the L there's the dining table and chairs, and then these lovely woven woollen rugs, which are made in the prisons, and you can buy those in the market – they're very attractive.

Unit 8   Get well soon

8A   How do you feel?

EXERCISE 2

1 I seem to have hurt my wrist.
2 I think it could be broken.
3 Thanks very much for coming in to see me.
4 Let me have a look at it, could I?
5 I think I'm fine, thanks very much.
6 I do remember falling over.

7 Perhaps you could just get me a copy of *Cosmopolitan* from the corner shop.
8 Hello, how can I help you?
9 I did go to a party last night.
10 I suppose I'd better be getting along.
11 Is there anything I can get you?
12 My advice is that you should go to the hospital and get it X-rayed.

EXERCISE 3

A) A: Well, I suppose I'd better be getting on . . .
   B: Well, thanks very much for coming in to see me.
   A: Not at all, as you know it's, it's no problem. Um, I mean is there anything I can get you or do for you?
   B: No, I think I'm fine, thanks very much.
   A: Are you sure?
   B: Yeah.
   A: Nothing at all?
   B: No. Oh, perhaps, perhaps you could just get me a copy of *Cosmopolitan* from the corner shop.
   A: Of course, yes. Fine. See you later.

B) A: Hello, how can I help you?
   B: Good morning. I seem to have hurt my wrist.
   A: Yes? How did you do that?
   B: Well, I'm not actually sure. I think . . . I did go to a party last night (*yes*) and um I sort of fell up the steps, you see (*yes*) and I may have done it then.
   A: You fell on it, you think?
   B: Well I think so. I do remember falling over.
   A: OK, let me have a look at it, could I? Yes, it is rather swollen. Does this hurt?
   B: Yes it does actually, yes.
   A: Yes, right, well my advice is that you should go to the hospital and get it X-rayed. I think it could be broken.

8B   Cures

EXERCISES 2 and 3

1 I simply fill up a glass of water, and, holding my breath, I take nine sips, not eight and not ten, but nine sips from the opposite side of the glass.
2 What you have to do is to have a friend with you who will hold your ears and press her fingers or his fingers into your ear-hole while you are drinking slowly from a full glass of water.

3 When you're feeling really bad, undress and get into bed. But before you actually get into bed, you must take a hat and put it at the foot of the bed. Then, you must have a bottle of brandy and a glass by your side. Take a glass of brandy and drink it. Drink another glass of brandy, and keep on drinking the brandy until you see three hats at the end of the bed. Then get a good night's sleep, and in the morning you'll be cured.

4 I was taken to the bathroom, and the sheet was taken from the bed, and the bath was filled with cold water. And the sheet was put in the cold water, I was undressed – and I had no clothes on – and I stood in the bathroom, and this wet, cold sheet was wrapped round me very tightly, with my arms to my side. Then I was put back on the bed, and within minutes I got hotter and hotter, and I started sweating.

Unit 9   What's going on?

9A   *What really happened?*

EXERCISES 2 and 3

A) A: Oops, oh sorry!
   B: Oh, do be careful!
   A: I said sorry.
   B: You've spilt it all down my dress.
   A: Well let me wipe it off. Sorry. (*OK*) At least it wasn't hot.

B) A: You will take care, won't you? The roads are very, very icy.
   B: Yes I know, don't worry. I'll drive very slowly. It'll be fine – don't worry about me.
   A: Well they've already reported some accidents on the radio this morning.
   B: I know. I will take care, I promise.

C) A: Do you like this dress? It's from my sister.
   B: I can tell it's from your sister.
   A: What do you mean?
   B: Well, she always sends you dresses that colour.
   A: Well, she makes them herself. I think they're lovely.
   B: Yes, but you look like a sack of potatoes in them.

9B   *Requests, offers and invitations*

EXERCISE 2

1 Well, I'd rather not if you don't mind. I'm sorry, it looks a bit heavy to me. (*A: Well, um*) I've got a bad back.

2 Oh I'm afraid I'm too busy at the moment. (*Oh*) I've got a big report to get done for tomorrow morning, and I'm – I think really I must, I must get that done.

3 Well I would, it's just that I'm supposed to be at the doctor's in five minutes, and I'm late as it is.

4 Oh no, don't worry. Thank you but you get off – I know you're in a hurry.

EXERCISE 3

A) A: Could you give me a hand moving this cupboard, please?
   B: Well, I'd rather not if you don't mind. I'm sorry, it looks a bit heavy to me. (*A: Well, um*) I've got a bad back.
   A: Oh have you? (*Yes*) I didn't realise.
   B: Yes, I'm not allowed to lift heavy things.
   A: Ah well. Well, let's see – perhaps we could get someone in from next door.
   B: Oh yes, Jim's next door, why don't you ask him? (*A: I thought he'd gone out*)

B) A: I was wondering – would you like to come to dinner tonight?
   B: Oh I'm afraid I'm too busy at the moment. (*Oh*) I've got a big report to get done for tomorrow morning, and I'm – I think really I must, I must get that done.
   A: What about tomorrow night, then?
   B: Um – yes, tomorrow night would be lovely.
   A: Oh, jolly good. (*Oh, thank you very much*) Lovely. About eight o'clock?
   B: Yes, that'll be fine. Thank you very much. (*Lovely*)

C) A: Excuse me, but I can't start my car. Do you think you could just help me give it a push?
   B: Well I would, it's just that I'm supposed to be at the doctor's in five minutes, and I'm late as it is.
   A: But it'll only take a moment.
   B: Oh well, OK, if it really is going to take a very short time. Where is it?

D) A: Do let me help you with the washing up.
   B: Oh no, don't worry. Thank you but you get off – I know you're in a hurry.
   A: Oh all right, well I will, then.
   B: I know one thing – could you possibly do something for me while you're out? I've run out of cash. Could you stop and get me some money at the bank?

Unit 10 Early one morning

10A The moment of waking

EXERCISE 2

I woke up and it was dark and stuffy. And there was the most terrible smell, it was a sort of cheesy smell, really bad cheese. And I couldn't think where I was. I shut my eyes and tried to remember where I was, and I realised I was very stiff and I could feel the floor rocking beneath me, and there was this sort of drumbeat noise. And it took me a few seconds to realise that I was in fact on the floor of a train. And I remembered – we were students, and there were eight of us in the compartment, and we'd decided that six people should sit on the seats with their legs up on the seat opposite, and two people should sleep on the floor under the legs, head to toe. And I realised I was under this sort of forest of legs, and the awful smell was my partner's feet which were right next to my face. And then I realised where I was, and you know after that it didn't seem so terrible.

EXERCISE 4

And I remembered – we were students, and there were eight of us in the compartment, and we'd decided that six people should sit on the seats with their legs up on the seat opposite, and two people should sleep on the floor under the legs, head to toe. And I realised I was under this sort of forest of legs, and the awful smell was my partner's feet which were right next to my face. And then I realised where I was, and you know after that it didn't seem so terrible.

10B Sights, sounds and smells

EXERCISE 2

I woke up very early in the morning, because there was a loud bell, and there was a sound of water rushing, and the engines of the boat were immediately underneath our very narrow beds. So all this noise came together, and it was a terrifying noise. And then we could hear breakfast and smell the breakfast being cooked. And I got up and walked along the passage, and there was an open stove, where a man was cooking a mass of bacon and eggs, but it was still very dark outside, and it was very cold, and there was a lot of mist, but it was very nice and warm and cosy there with a lot of people drinking tea out of metal cups, and waiting for their very early hot breakfast.

EXERCISE 3

1 I woke up very early in the morning.
2 And the engines of the boat were immediately underneath our very narrow beds.
3 All this noise came together and it was a terrifying noise.
4 I got up and walked along the passage.
5 There was an open stove, where a man was cooking a mass of bacon and eggs.
6 It was still very dark outside and it was very cold, and there was a lot of mist.
7 But it was very nice and warm and cosy there.

Unit 11 Presents

11A Envelope

EXERCISE 3

A: Go on. Open it.
B: Right. (laughs)
A: Go on.
B: It's not very big. You've already given me a card. (Yes) It's just like another card. Now, let's see . . . Now then . . . What? What is it? Oh no, this is ridiculous. (Laughter) This must have cost you a fortune.
A: No it didn't.
B: Well, I hope you're coming too.
A: I am!
B: Bombay! A ticket to Bombay!

11B Presents for the family

EXERCISE 1

I had gone to stay with a family in France when I was a student. •
I had gone to stay with a family in France when I was a student and I took with me some presents for the family I was going to stay with and gave them to the lady of the house and the members of the family when I arrived.

EXERCISE 2

I stayed there for a fortnight and I had a wonderful time. •
I stayed there for a fortnight and I had a wonderful time, and at the end of my stay I went out to the shops and I bought presents to take back to my mother and father and my brother and my aunt and other relatives.

EXERCISE 3

And when I came back to the house the little

girl who lived in the house asked me what I had bought and what was in my bag. ●
And when I came back to the house the little girl who lived in the house asked me what I had bought and what was in my bag. So I opened the bag and I began to take everything out, and I was standing in the middle of the dining room with a big box of chocolates in my hand – the chocolates were actually for my aunt – when the lady of the house came into the room.

EXERCISE 4

And she said, 'Oh, you shouldn't have! You've already bought enough – really. It wasn't necessary'. And of course my face just went bright red, I couldn't think of anything to say. I just looked at her, I put the box of chocolates down on the table and I fled from the room.

Unit 12   Small talk

12A   Party guests

EXERCISES 2 and 3

A: Christian!
B: Hello, John.
A: Marvellous to see you!
B: Yeah, it's great to see you. I'm sorry I'm late. I got held up at the airport.
A: Don't worry. Look, let me introduce you to a very good friend who's also my neighbour – lives next door. Adrienne – Christian.
B: Hello, how d'you do? Hi!
C: Nice to meet you.
B: Yeah, you too. Yeah.
A: Well, can I get you both a drink?
C: Oh yes please, that would be lovely.

12B   Coffee morning

EXERCISES 1 and 3

A: Well, I'd better be getting home.
B: Oh, must you?
C: I must, too. (*Afraid so*) It's been great seeing you again.
B: Oh, it was marvellous seeing you, and so unexpected.
A: Oh it's all right, we were just passing by. Thanks for the coffee, by the way – delicious.
B: Pleasure. (*Yes*)
A: Maybe we can meet up some time next week or . . .?
B: Well yes, why not, yes. When are you free?
C: Tuesday?
A: Tuesday would be fine.

Unit 13   Van Gogh

13A   Van Gogh's chair

EXERCISE 2

The main theme of the picture seems to be a big chair, and a pipe and some tobacco lying on this chair. And it seems that there is really nothing else happening in this picture, but it is not true, because you really can feel the presence of a man who left this pipe on this chair, and who just went out to do something else and will be back in a minute and pick up this pipe and smoke it.

I love the colours, which are typical Van Gogh colours – very clear colours, very bright ones. The chair is yellow, and it is set against the blue background of the wall, and it is standing on the floor which is made of red tiles. And those three colours seem to dominate the picture.

13B   Your own chair

EXERCISE 2

1 Well, my chair would be a lovely big armchair, a very comfortable chair, and on it would be several cushions. And also on the arm of the chair would be the remote control for my television and, and video, as I do watch the television a lot, and that's the way I often relax. But one thing I've missed out is usually on the chair with me would be my black and white cat, and he would most definitely be on the chair as well.
2 My chair would be a large wooden rocking chair, with all sorts of cushions to make it soft and comfortable, and over one arm there'd be a copy of the newspaper, probably open on the page where the crossword is. And at the foot of the, of the rocking chair there'd be a bowl of fruit, because I like sitting down eating oranges doing the crossword.
3 My chair, would be a metal black kitchen chair, and on the chair would be an open book – a cookery book, because I like to cook, and also I'd probably have a tea-towel draped over the back of the chair.
4 My chair would be a large old Victorian leather armchair, the sort that makes a squeak when you sit into it. And on it, on the side, on the arm would be a packet of cigarettes and a lighter. On the other arm would probably be a half-finished box of chocolates.

EXERCISE 3

1 My chair would be a large wooden rocking chair, with all sorts of cushions to make it soft and comfortable.
2 And also I'd probably have a tea-towel draped over the back of the chair.
3 And also on the arm of the chair would be the remote control for my television and video.
4 My chair would be a large old Victorian leather armchair, the sort that makes a squeak when you sit into it.

Unit 14   Two towns

14A   Street scene

EXERCISE 2

I woke in the morning and everything was already in full swing in the streets. It was about half past ten, eleven o'clock. I walked out onto the balcony, and looked down, and the streets were full of people, absolutely full of people, and of cars, and of donkeys, and dogs and various other animals. There was a garage just below the flat, so there was a tremendous amount of noise coming from that. A lot of little shops, one shop selling chickens and hens, turkeys, rabbits, and so there was noise from that. A lot of different smells – of fruit and vegetables, of cooking, um, some not very pleasant smells, as it's, it's quite a dirty city, so quite a lot of petrol in the air, and industrial smoke. But on the whole, lovely smells.

14B   A town in Wales

EXERCISE 1

This is a very small, busy town that doesn't have very many tourists, and it's in the middle of Wales, and it's a very grey town to look at. The stone is grey of the houses, the shops look grey, the bridge is grey, everything is grey, but the people are very friendly. And they love talking on the street and finding out the news, the news about everybody who lives near the town and in the town. So that if you break your leg, everybody in the town knows before the ambulance has reached the hospital and it's er very friendly and very nice, and people are very kind.

EXERCISE 2

But Monday was the big day in the town, because that was the day of the farming sale – the market, when the farmers would bring

down mostly sheep. And in the old days they would start out very early in the morning and drive the sheep through the countryside and through the streets of the town to the market. But nowadays mostly it's done by very large lorries. But you still see hundreds and hundreds of sheep being chased through the main street of the town and behind the main shops into the market place. And the noise of hundreds of sheep in those small town streets is incredibly noisy.

Unit 15   Air travel

15A   In the air

EXERCISE 3

A) Oh, I had the most wonderful time. I was a bit frightened at first, especially when we first went up – it was so noisy. Well then I got used to it, and I spent all the time looking out over the countryside and the fields – oh it was lovely.

B) Well, I was absolutely terrified, but there was no turning back now. They opened the door and pushed me out, and I just floated down through the air and looked round at everything, and it was the most wonderful experience I've ever had.

C) Once there was enough wind I let my skis run on the snow and I took off. And it was amazing seeing far below in the valley the houses and the river. I didn't fly for very long – probably no more than ten or fifteen seconds – but it seemed much much longer.

D) Well, my friend John was the pilot, and I sat behind him, and we took off and then suddenly we were up there and it was a wonderful view. And I was surprised how, how noisy it was really. And we flew around for a little while, and then came in for what I have to admit was a rather bumpy landing.

EXERCISE 5

A) 1 Oh, I had the most wonderful time.
   2 I was a bit frightened at first.
   3 I spent all the time looking out over the countryside and the fields.

B) 1 And it was the most wonderful experience I've ever had.
   2 They opened the door and pushed me out.
   3 I just floated down through the air and looked round at everything.

C) 1 I let my skis run on the snow and I took off.
   2 And it was amazing seeing far below in the valley the houses and the river.
   3 I didn't fly for very long – probably no more than ten or fifteen seconds.

D) 1 My friend John was the pilot, and I sat behind him.
   2 I was surprised how noisy it was really.
   3 I have to admit was a rather bumpy landing.

15B Airport

EXERCISES 1 and 2

1 This is the final call for passengers travelling on British Airways Flight BA 653 to New York and Washington. Will remaining passengers for this flight please go to Gate No. 3.
2 Here is an announcement. Pan American Flight PA 241 has been delayed until further notice. Passengers for this flight should remain in the departure lounge.
3 Attention all passengers. Please keep your baggage with you at all times. If you see any unattended bags or suitcases, please report them immediately to the airport staff. Thank you.
4 Would Mr Alomba, joining Flight EA 242 to Addis Ababa, please go immediately to Gate No. 6.
5 Would Ms Joanne Underhill, a passenger travelling to New York, please come to the Information Desk on the second floor.
6 Here is an announcement. A wallet has been found belonging to Mr John Underwood. Would Mr Underwood please come to the Information Desk. Thank you.
7 Will all passengers for Pan American Flight PA 241 to New York, proceed to Gate No. 3. This flight is now boarding.

Unit 16 Tarantula

16A One day in California . . .

EXERCISES 3 and 4

A: Tell me about the time that you met a tarantula.
B: Well, I was in Southern California and I was trying to be a real Southern Californian and I was jogging home across the the sandhills and, as I jogged along the path, I noticed something jogging towards me and it was a giant tarantula and it was all black and hairy and I walked up to it and it walked up to me and we looked at each other and I thought 'I should pick this up, I should be a brave person 'cause this isn't going to hurt me' and I couldn't bear to pick it up. I just couldn't, I sort of walked gently around it and I ran away (*laughter*).

16B Fear of spiders

EXERCISE 2

A: Why do you think people are afraid of tarantulas?
B: Well, I guess it's because people are afraid of all spiders and tarantulas happen to be pretty much the biggest of all the spiders. And maybe it's also because some spiders really are very poisonous. In California for example – living in most of the garages in California – you get black widow spiders, which are quite small but they're certainly more dangerous than tarantulas.
A: But personally you aren't afraid of tarantulas?
B: Well I shouldn't be frightened of tarantulas, simply because I know that they aren't really dangerous – all they can do is give you a small bite, but it's not poisonous. And yet I must say I don't like to pick them up. But you see, some people keep pet mice and pet rabbits and, well they can give you a much worse bite than a tarantula ever could. And yet people aren't frightened of them.

EXERCISE 3

A: Why do you think people are frightened of spiders?
B: I don't know – it's very strange. People are frightened of spiders and they are frightened of snakes, and, well obviously some spiders and some snakes really are poisonous. But most snakes are harmless, and it's really strange that people are so frightened of spiders because it's quite difficult to find a spider that's really dangerous.

EXERCISE 4

B: But obviously some people aren't afraid of spiders, because in America, if you look in the pet shops you can see tarantulas for sale. So obviously some people think that they are nice friendly little creatures and they really like them.

Unit 17   Customs

17A   *Japanese bath*

EXERCISE 2

First of all you fill some cold water in a bath tub. You put the lid on the bath, then you switch the gas on. Then you get undressed and um you sort of take the lid off the bath. Now once you get into the bath, you sit there, and sort of relax. Then you get out of the bath, and there's always a little stool to sit on. Now you always get hot water from the bath, not from a tap. Then you soap your sponge, then start washing from your top towards the bottom. Then you rinse – again take water from the bath tub, and pour it over, and rinse your body thoroughly. Then you start washing your hair. After you've made sure that your body is no longer soapy, and your hair is no longer soapy and everything, you then get back into the bath. And then you just sit in the bath, again just relaxing. Then you get out, and then dry yourself and then put nice clean clothes on.

17B   *Christmas in Poland*

EXERCISE 2

People tend to spend Christmas with your closest relatives, and the most important point of Christmas is Christmas Eve supper. And the whole family just gathers around the table, and there are twelve traditional dishes on the table, and you are supposed to taste them all, because if you don't try any of them you may face some misfortune in the following year. Well, before everybody sits down to eat the supper, we just break wafers with each other, wishing each other good luck. When the supper is over the children go to the other room, where the big Christmas tree stands, and they find some Christmas presents under the Christmas tree. And after the supper, the whole family just sit around the table singing Christmas carols, and waiting for midnight, when they go to church.

EXERCISE 3

1 The most important point of Christmas is Christmas Eve supper.
2 There are twelve traditional dishes on the table.
3 You are supposed to taste them all.
4 Because if you don't try any of them you may face some misfortune in the following year.
5 The children go to the other room, where the big Christmas tree stands, and they find some Christmas presents under the Christmas tree.
6 Waiting for midnight, when they go to church.

Unit 18   How to do it

18A   *Origami*

EXERCISE 1

First of all, you fold the paper in half, and then open it again. And then you fold it in half the other way, and open it again. ●
   Then you fold each of the corners into the centre, so that you have a smaller square. ●
   Now you've got a smaller square, so then you fold the top two sides into the centre, and that should make the top part look like a triangle. ●
   And then if you fold up the bottom, it makes a triangle. ●
   And then next you fold in the bottom two corners towards the centre. ●
   Then you fold the bottom up, to about half way up the triangle. And then fold half of it back down again, now that should make the frog's feet. ●
   Then you fold the top corner down, just a little way, and that makes his head. ●
   Then if you turn the frog over, and you press on the frog's back with your finger, you can make him jump.

18B   *Press this button . . .*

EXERCISE 1

1 Put the lid on and turn it round, OK? You just turn it until it clicks, right? Now put the carrot in there, in the funnel, and put that on the top so you can push the carrot down. And then you just turn that knob to the right, and that starts it.
2 OK, well get the piece of wood, put it down on the table and hold it down, hard as you can, that's right. Then get the saw, and see the mark on the piece of wood? Just put it on the mark, and then very slowly just pull it towards you and then push it back, and pull it towards you and push it back, just very gently.
3 Take the key and put it into the keyhole, just there, right? Make sure that you're in neutral, and then turn the key, and first of all a red light should come on – that's right. And then turn it again, and, as you do, press down on the accelerator.
4 Sit with your back straight, and your fingers out in front of the keys. Your right thumb over the middle of the keyboard, and also

your left thumb in the same place. Your fingers out in front of you – yeah, a little bit more. And that's fine.

EXERCISES 2 and 4

1 Put the lid on and turn it round, OK? You just turn it until it clicks, right? Now put the carrot in there, in the funnel, and put that on the top so you can push the carrot down. And then you just turn that knob to the right, and that starts it. (*Sound of food processor*)
2 OK, well get the piece of wood, put it down on the table and hold it down, hard as you can, that's right. Then get the saw, and see the mark on the piece of wood? Just put it on the mark, and then very slowly just pull it towards you and then push it back, and pull it towards you and push it back, just very gently. (*Sound of sawing wood*)
3 Take the key and put it into the keyhole, just there, right? Make sure that you're in neutral, and then turn the key, and first of all a red light should come on – that's right. And then turn it again, and, as you do, press down on the accelerator. (*Sound of car engine*)
4 Sit with your back straight, and your fingers out in front of the keys. Your right thumb over the middle of the keyboard, and also your left thumb in the same place. Your fingers out in front of you – yeah, a little bit more. And that's fine. (*Sound of piano*)

Unit 19   People at work

19A   A working day

EXERCISE 2

Yeah well it was a good day, really. We had to put a new window in. The weather was good, so we didn't have any problems there. Anyway, we got the hole knocked out by about lunchtime, put in the new window, got the glass, and managed to get in a coat of paint before we came home this evening.

EXERCISES 3 and 4

Yes, I had rather a good day, really. I had five tests in all, and three out of five passed. Um, I was a bit worried at first, because the first person nearly ran over a policeman. But er the next three were all right, no problems. Oh yeah, the last one it must be the fifteenth time he's taken the test, and he went through two sets of

traffic lights. I felt very sorry for him, but I had to fail him again.

19B   Round the table

EXERCISE 2

A: Sorry I'm late. The traffic was terrible.
B: It's all right, don't worry, we haven't started yet.
A: I thought I'd never make the meeting. It was really bad this morning, wasn't it?
C: Was it? Where were you?
A: Coming down that main road (*Oh*), where the traffic lights are jammed.
C: Yes, well I tried to avoid that. Of course, everyone else tried to avoid it, and I got into another jam. Where's the chairman?
B: I suppose he's somewhere in the middle of it all, at this very moment.
C: Well, do you think we should wait for him?
B: I think we'd better, don't you?

EXERCISE 3

A: Sorry I'm late. The traffic was terrible. •
B: It's all right, don't worry, we haven't started yet. •
A: I thought I'd never make the meeting. It was really bad this morning, wasn't it? •
C: Was it? Where were you?
A: Coming down that main road (*Oh*), where the traffic lights are jammed. •
C: Yes, well I tried to avoid that. Of course, everyone else tried to avoid it, and I got into another jam. • Where's the chairman?
B: I suppose he's somewhere in the middle of it all, at this very moment. •
C: Well, do you think we should wait for him?
B: I think we'd better, don't you?

Unit 20   Holidays

20A   Holiday photos

EXERCISE 4

1 And they were preparing this huge breakfast.
2 And here we are going up the side of another mountain.
3 It was very difficult with the pushchair on those stony paths.
4 She would sit there cooking lamb on charcoal.
5 You can see that big plate of kebabs and mint tea.
6 She's got my daughter Anna on her knee.

EXERCISE 5

A) This photo is in Goulimine, in Morocco. That – and it's the morning, and it was already incredibly hot, and they were preparing this huge breakfast. You can see that big plate of kebabs and mint tea. And, we ate all of it because it was delicious.

B) This was a little taverna right on the beach, and this girl's name was Poppy and she would sit there cooking lamb on charcoal every day and all day. And, um, she's got my daughter Anna on her knee. And we used to go there most evenings, and that lamb was wonderful.

C) And here we are going up the side of another mountain, and you can see the boys racing off in front. They were, oh they loved it, they were always miles ahead and I was always miles behind. It was very difficult with the pushchair, on those stony paths.

20B The Seychelles

EXERCISES 2 and 3

We flew to Mahé, which is the largest of the islands in the Seychelles, and immediately got a small plane to the second biggest island, which is called Praslin. It's still pretty small, I think it's about ten miles in diameter, so a small place. It really was like a perfect story-book island, with coral reefs and white sand and perfect temperature. The other extraordinary thing about Praslin is it has an ancient primeval forest called the Valley de Maie. This forest hasn't been touched for millions of years. And we went to a lot of other little islands while we were there, mostly on boats. We went to an extraordinary island called Curieuse, which used to be a leper colony, and has a large amount of giant tortoises, and they really are big, a small child could ride on one of these tortoises. We also went to Cousin Island, and that is a bird sanctuary, and has beautiful birds. We then travelled to Denis Island for one week, which is a private island, which just has a hotel and you really feel as if you are Robinson Crusoe on this island, with these beautiful perfect coral reefs, and this blue–green sea, and the lagoons.

To the teacher

This book has two main aims:
- to provide *opportunities* to listen to a wide variety of natural spoken English, presented in a way that is accessible to learners at a pre-intermediate level.
- to develop students' listening *skills* by helping them to draw on their own natural strategies for listening effectively.

Listening strategies

A fundamental idea underlying this book is that listening is not merely a 'passive' or 'receptive' skill; rather that when we listen we naturally employ a variety of active 'strategies' which help us to make sense of what we are listening to.

These strategies include:
- making predictions about what the speaker is going to say next or where the discourse is 'leading to';
- matching what we hear against our own experience, knowledge of the world, and preconceptions;
- trying to visualise elements of what we hear, and form a mental picture that corresponds roughly to that of the speaker;
- distinguishing the main point of what we hear from less important details, and 'following the thread' of a conversation or anecdote;
- listening out for particular points of detail that are especially relevant to us;
- responding intellectually and emotionally to what we hear: agreeing or disagreeing, approving or disapproving, being surprised, disturbed, amused, etc.;
- inferring information about the speakers and their situation that is implied in what we hear.

We had these strategies very much in mind while developing the units that make up this book, and they are referred to in the Map of the book on pages 6–7. We have not regarded these strategies as discrete 'skills' that can or need to be taught; we have seen them rather as an underlying resource that students already have in their own language, and have tried to develop exercises which encourage students to draw on them to help them listen to English.

The recordings

Natural spontaneous speech is quite different in its structure from scripted monologue or dialogue – as well as showing greater redundancy and often including more hesitation, there are important differences in rhythm and in the way speakers use pausing to divide up their message. Because of these differences, we feel that scripted recordings cannot adequately prepare students for listening to the natural language they will encounter in the real world. Consequently, nearly all the recordings for this book are of spontaneous, unscripted language; some of the material is taken from authentic informal interviews, and some is improvised by actors.

We have tried to include a variety of voices and speaking styles in the book. So as not to burden elementary listeners with unnecessary difficulties, most speakers in the recordings use some variety of 'standard British English', although the material also includes some modified regional accents as well as non-native speakers of English (in Units 13 and 17).

Grading

Although we have selected recordings that do not have too heavy a lexical or structural load, we have avoided using 'simplicity of language' as our only criterion in grading the material. Instead, we have left the language as natural as possible and tried to incorporate other features into the book to bring the level down and make it accessible to learners at a pre-intermediate level:
- Especially in the earlier units, the stretches of speech that students listen to at a time are kept quite short, and can easily be played several times over.
- Longer pieces of listening are usually divided into shorter sections, each with its own listening task.
- In many units, particular utterances have been rerecorded separately so that they can be listened to in isolation, either before or after the main listening activity; we hope that this helps to overcome the sense of panic that learners are liable to feel when listening to an apparently 'unstoppable' stream of language.
- In most of the recordings students only have to listen to one person speaking, although some units (e.g. 9B, 12, 19B) intentionally introduce conversations between two or more speakers in order to focus on this as a comprehension feature.
- We have made extensive use of pre-listening activities, in which students are encouraged to make predictions about what they are going to hear. This not only helps to focus on the topic but it greatly simplifies the listening task by making the message more predictable.

Using the book

Structure of the book

Each unit is divided into two parts, A and B. Each part provides material for 30–45 minutes of class listening and associated activities. Usually the two parts of the unit are independent of each other, reflecting different aspects of one topic; in a few units (4, 13, 16) the two parts develop a single idea and so belong more closely together. This structure is intended to make the material as flexible as possible: one part of any unit can be used on its own or the two parts can be used together.

Listening in class

The book is mainly designed to be used in class, and this is reflected in the active approach we have taken to listening. Although the main focus of each unit is on listening, this is integrated into a range of oral (and sometimes written) activities. Each section begins with a pre-listening activity, to introduce the topic and prepare students for the listening; most of the listening tasks themselves are open-ended, to encourage students to discuss, comment, interpret and react, as well as merely record information; and the listening stage is followed by an extension activity in which students can use what they have listened to as a basis for creative speaking and writing.

Self-study listening

Although the book is mainly intended for use in class, many of the activities can be done by students working alone with the cassette, either at home or in a self-access room or language laboratory, using the tapescript at the end of the book as an answer key. As each unit is divided into two sections, it would also be possible to cover the first half of each unit in class, and leave the second half for students to work through on their own outside class time.

We hope this book will help your students to listen to English effectively, and that both you and they enjoy using the material.